MUFFINS, TEA BREADS & GEMS

By
Sherri Eldridge

GW00706083

Illustrations by
Rob Groves

Muffins, Tea Breads & Gems

Published by:
Harvest Hill Press
Post Office Box 55
Salisbury Cove, Maine 04672
207-288-8900

ISBN: 1-886862-27-3

First printing: August 1998
Second printing: August 2001
Third printing: April 2002
Fourth printing: June 2003
Fifth printing: April 2006

PRINTED IN CANADA
ON ACID-FREE PAPER

The recipes in this book were created with the goal of reducing fat, calories, cholesterol and sodium. They also present a variety of fresh healthy foods, to be prepared with love and eaten with pleasure.

CREDITS:

Cover border from cotton print gratefully used as a courtesy of:
Hoffman International Fabrics

Cover Design, Layout and Typesetting: Sherri Eldridge

Front Cover Watercolor and Text Line Art: Robert Groves

Text Typesetting and Proofreading: Bill Eldridge

PREFACE

The story of quick breads began with the development and use of baking soda 150 years ago. Baking soda and baking powder chemically generate carbon dioxide, causing bread to rise. Before the mid-1800s, bread required the slow biological action of yeast to raise the dough.

Muffins, tea breads and gems are called quick breads because they can be baked as soon as the dough is made. The two kinds of quick bread are batter breads and dough breads. Batter breads are only briefly mixed together and include muffins, gems, coffee cakes, popovers, tea breads, corn bread, spoon bread, brown and soda breads. Dough breads include scones and biscuits. They need oil to be cut into the flour and kneading to bring the ingredients together.

Muffins, Tea Breads & Gems presents both the sweet and savory batter breads. Savory Chile and Cheese Muffins served with a plate of chiles relleños makes a dinner, and a sweet Blueberry Streusel Muffin is perfect for breakfast. The savory Sun-dried Tomato and Garlic Bread complements scrambled eggs, while the sweet Rose Garden Bread is ideal for afternoon tea.

Quick bread recipes lend themselves to our busy schedules. You can quickly make them for family, company or just for yourself. Make a batch, freeze some batter for later, and you can always enjoy the fresh-baked flavor of your favorite bread!

CONTENTS

Pineapple Upside-Down Muffins

MAKES 12 MUFFINS

1 cup pineapple preserves
1 egg
1 cup nonfat buttermilk
3 tablespoons canola oil
2 tablespoons honey
1 teaspoon vanilla extract
1¾ cups all-purpose flour
½ cup packed brown sugar
1 tablespoon baking powder
¼ teaspoon baking soda
¼ teaspoon salt
¼ teaspoon cinnamon

Serving: 1 Muffin
Protein: 3 gm
Carbs: 44 gm
Sodium: 151 mg

Calories: 209
Fat: 3 gm
Cholesterol: 18 mg
Calcium: 65 mg

Preheat oven to 400°. Spray a large muffin tin with nonstick oil. Spoon a large tablespoon of pineapple preserves into the bottom of each muffin tin. This will use about ¾ cup of the preserves.

In a mixing bowl, beat egg, buttermilk, oil, honey, ¼ cup pineapple preserves and vanilla until blended.

In a large bowl, stir together flour, sugar, baking powder, baking soda, salt and cinnamon. With a few quick strokes, combine dry and liquid mixtures. Fill muffin cups ¾ full. Bake 25 minutes, or until a toothpick inserted into the middle muffin comes out clean. Turn out from pan immediately, or preserves will stick to muffin cups. Cool on wire rack for 5 minutes, serve warm.

Apricot Bran Muffins

1 egg
1 ¼ cups buttermilk
2 tablespoons canola oil
¼ cup honey
1 tablespoon molasses
1 teaspoon almond extract
1 ¼ cups shredded
    100% all-bran cereal
1 ¼ cups all-purpose flour
1 tablespoon baking powder
½ teaspoon baking soda
pinch of salt
1 cup dried apricots
    diced into ¼" cubes
1 tablespoon flour

Serving: 1 Muffin
Protein: 4 gm
Carbs: 30 gm
Sodium: 214 mg

Calories: 153
Fat: 3 gm
Cholesterol: 18 mg
Calcium: 65 mg

MAKES 12 MUFFINS

Preheat oven to 400°. Spray a large muffin tin with nonstick oil.

In a bowl, beat egg, buttermilk, oil, honey, molasses and almond extract until well blended. Add bran cereal and soak 5 minutes.

In a large mixing bowl, stir flour, baking powder, baking soda and salt until well blended. With a few quick strokes, combine dry and liquid mixtures. Toss apricot pieces with tablespoon of flour, then gently fold into batter. Fill muffin cups ¾ full. Bake for 20 minutes, or until a toothpick inserted into the center of muffins comes out clean.

Cool for 5 minutes in pan, serve warm.

Strawberry Surprise Muffins

1 egg
1 egg white
1 cup buttermilk
2 tablespoons canola oil
¼ cup honey
1 teaspoon vanilla extract
finely grated rind of 1 lemon
2 cups all-purpose flour
4 tablespoons sugar
1 tablespoon baking powder
¼ teaspoon salt
¼ cup strawberry preserves

Serving: 1 Muffin
Protein: 3 gm
Carbs: 35 gm
Sodium: 170 mg

Calories: 180
Fat: 3 gm
Cholesterol: 18 mg
Calcium: 55 mg

MAKES 12 MUFFINS

Preheat oven to 400°. Spray a large muffin tin with nonstick oil.

In a bowl, beat egg, egg white, buttermilk, oil, honey, vanilla and lemon rind until well blended.

In a large mixing bowl, combine flour, 2 tablespoons sugar, baking powder and salt. With a few quick strokes, mix together dry and liquid mixtures. Fill muffin cups half full. Make a small indentation in center of each muffin and fill with 2 teaspoons strawberry preserves. Cover each muffin evenly with remaining batter. Sprinkle tops with remaining 2 tablespoons sugar. Bake 20 minutes, or until a toothpick inserted into the middle comes out clean.

Perfect Peach Muffins

1 egg
1 egg white
2 tablespoons canola oil
1 teaspoon vanilla extract
finely grated rind of an
    orange
1 cup peach purée
    (see instructions)
2 cups all-purpose flour
¾ cup sugar
1 tablespoon baking powder
½ teaspoon baking soda
¼ teaspoon salt

Serving: 1 Muffin
Protein: 3 gm
Carbs: 31 gm
Sodium: 163 mg

Calories: 163
Fat: 3 gm
Cholesterol: 18 mg
Calcium: 48 mg

MAKES 12 MUFFINS

Preheat oven to 400°. Spray a large muffin tin with nonstick oil.

In a mixing bowl, beat egg, egg white, oil, vanilla and orange rind until well blended. Beat in peach purée.

In a large bowl, stir flour, sugar, baking powder, baking soda and salt until well blended. With a few quick strokes, combine dry and liquid mixtures. Fill muffin cups ¾ full. Bake 20 minutes or until a toothpick inserted into the middle comes out clean. Cool for 5 minutes in pan, and serve warm.

Peach Purée: Select 3 ripe peaches. Score an "X" into the top and bottom of each, place in boiling water 10 minutes. Drain, then cool in ice water. Skins will now easily peel off. Dice peaches, place in blender, pulse briefly to purée.

Carrot Poppy Seed Muffins

1½ cups finely grated peeled
carrots, loosely packed
¾ cup packed brown sugar
3 tablespoons honey
1 teaspoon lemon juice
1 teaspoon baking soda
3 tablespoons canola oil
3 tablespoons poppy seeds
1 cup boiling water
2 cups all-purpose flour
2 teaspoons baking powder
1 teaspoon cinnamon

Serving: 1 Muffin
Protein: 3 gm
Carbs: 36 gm
Sodium: 184 mg

Calories: 191
Fat: 4.5 gm
Cholesterol: 0 mg
Calcium: 79 mg

MAKES 12 MUFFINS

Preheat oven to 350°. Spray muffin tins with nonstick oil.

In a large bowl, combine grated carrots, sugar, honey, lemon juice, baking soda, oil, poppy seeds and boiling water. Let rest at least 10 minutes.

In a separate bowl, mix flour, baking powder and cinnamon. After carrot mixture has rested, stir in flour mixture just until moistened (do not over mix). Fill muffin cups ¾ full. Bake 30-35 minutes, or until toothpick inserted in muffins comes out clean. Remove tin from oven but leave muffins in tins another 10 minutes before cooling on wire rack.

Know Your Ingredients

Making a quick bread requires flour, a liquid, and eggs or another item to hold the batter. The leavening agent causes breads to rise and be light. Non-wheat grains, fats, sugars and fillings add flavor.

Flours are generally white or whole wheat. White flours contain only the wheat berry endosperm, while whole wheat also includes the bran and germ. Bran is a source of insoluble fiber. Wheat germ contains polyunsaturated oils, iron and vitamins B and E. All-purpose flour has protein levels midway between cake and bread flour. White flour that is unbleached and finely ground from hard red wheat is the best for baking.

Baking soda and baking powder deteriorate over time, so replace them after 6 months. Baking soda needs an acid such as buttermilk, yogurt or fruit juice to work. A half teaspoon of baking soda used with an acid is an equivalent substitute for two tablespoons of baking powder. Baking powder is a combination of baking soda and a fruit acid, and starts to work as soon as it is wet. For high-altitude baking, reduce baking powder or soda by 25%. You can substitute whipped egg whites for whole eggs, but leave at least one yolk in the recipe. To lower saturated fats, use canola oil in place of butter or lard. Because fat reduction may result in less flavor, a little salt can be added to the recipe.

Blueberry Streusel Muffins

1 egg
1 egg white
3 tablespoons canola oil
1 cup nonfat sour cream
2 tablespoons finely grated
    lemon rind
2 cups all-purpose flour
1 cup packed brown sugar
1 tablespoon baking powder
½ teaspoon cinnamon
¼ teaspoon salt
1 cup blueberries tossed
    with 2 tablespoons flour
¼ cup sugar

Serving: 1 Muffin
Protein: 5 gm
Carbs: 45 gm
Sodium: 235 mg

Calories: 234
Fat: 4 gm
Cholesterol: 18 mg
Calcium: 131 mg

MAKES 12 MUFFINS

Preheat oven to 400°. Spray a large muffin tin with nonstick oil.

In a bowl, beat egg, egg white, oil, sour cream and 1 tablespoon grated lemon rind.

In a large bowl, stir flour, brown sugar, baking powder, cinnamon and salt until well blended. With a few quick strokes, combine dry and liquid mixtures. Gently fold blueberries into batter. Fill muffin cups ¾ full. Mix remaining tablespoon lemon rind and sugar, then sprinkle 1 teaspoon over top of each muffin Bake for 20 minutes or until a toothpick inserted into the middle comes out clean.

Cool for 5 minutes and serve warm.

Honey Gingerbread Muffins

½ cup packed brown sugar
3 tablespoons canola oil
1 egg
1 egg white
¼ cup honey
¼ cup molasses
2½ cups all-purpose flour
1½ teaspoons baking soda
½ teaspoon ground allspice
1 teaspoon ground ginger
1 teaspoon cinnamon
pinch of salt
1 cup boiling water
¼ cup golden raisins tossed
     with 1 teaspoon flour

Serving: 1 Muffin
Protein: 4 gm
Carbs: 42 gm
Sodium: 185 mg

Calories: 217
Fat: 4 gm
Cholesterol: 18 mg
Calcium: 33 mg

MAKES 12 MUFFINS

Preheat oven to 400°. Spray a large muffin tin with nonstick oil.

In a bowl, cream brown sugar and oil. Beat in egg, egg white, honey and molasses until well blended.

In a large bowl, mix together flour, baking soda, allspice, ginger, cinnamon and salt. With a few quick strokes, combine liquid blend, dry mixture and boiling water. Gently fold raisins into batter. Fill muffin cups ¾ full. Bake 20 minutes or until a toothpick inserted into the center of muffins comes out clean. Cool 5 minutes and serve warm.

Banana Pecan Muffins

1 cup sugar
2 tablespoons canola oil
1 egg
1 egg white
½ cup nonfat sour cream
1 teaspoon vanilla extract
1 cup mashed ripe bananas
2 cups all-purpose flour
2 teaspoons baking powder
1 teaspoon baking soda
pinch of salt
¼ cup chopped pecans
     tossed in 1 teaspoon flour

Serving: 1 Muffin
Protein: 3 gm
Carbs: 32 gm
Sodium: 200 mg

Calories: 177
Fat: 4.5 gm
Cholesterol: 18 mg
Calcium: 46 mg

MAKES 12 MUFFINS

Preheat oven to 400°. Spray a large muffin tin with nonstick oil.

In a bowl, cream sugar and oil. Beat in egg, egg white, sour cream, vanilla and bananas until well blended.

In a large bowl, stir together flour, baking powder, baking soda and salt. With a few quick strokes, combine dry and liquid mixtures. Gently fold pecans into batter. Fill muffin cups ¾ full. Bake for 20 minutes or until a toothpick inserted into the middle comes out clean.

Cool for 5 minutes and serve warm.

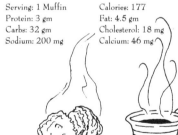

Chile and Cheese Muffins

1 egg
¾ cup skim milk
1½ tablespoons canola oil
½ cup canned creamed corn
1 tablespoon sugar
1¼ cups all-purpose flour
1 tablespoon baking powder
pinch of salt
pinch of cayenne
1 cup yellow cornmeal
¾ cup grated lowfat
  cheddar cheese
½ cup chopped green chiles
2 tablespoons minced red
  bell pepper
3 tablespoons salsa
1 teaspoon dried cilantro

MAKES 12 MUFFINS

Preheat oven to 400°. Spray a large muffin tin with nonstick oil.

In a bowl, beat egg, milk, oil and creamed corn until well blended.

In a large bowl, mix sugar, flour, baking powder, salt, cayenne and cornmeal. With a few quick strokes, combine dry and liquid mixtures.

In another bowl, mix cheese, chiles, pepper, salsa and cilantro, then gently fold into batter. Fill cups ¾ full. Bake for 20 minutes, or until a toothpick inserted into the middle comes out clean.

Serving: 1 Muffin
Protein: 6 gm
Carbs: 22 gm
Sodium: 168 mg

Calories: 144
Fat: 3 gm
Cholesterol: 20 mg
Calcium: 144 mg

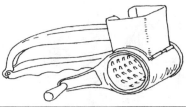

All About Muffins

Gems preceded muffins in culinary history. A gem pan has space for 12 gems and is similar in shape to today's muffin tins, except it is made of cast iron. The use of iron distributes the heat evenly and causes the entire gem to brown, similar to a popover.

Muffin batters are easily made. The dry and liquid ingredients are mixed separately. A light stirring of the dry ingredients into the liquid for 10 to 20 seconds is sufficient. Too much mixing toughens the muffin. There will be lumps in the batter; just ignore them. Gently fold any fruit or nuts into the batter with a spatula. Any muffin recipe can be used for coffee cake and vice versa.

Oven heat is very important. Always preheat the oven and resist the temptation to open the oven doors before their time. If the top of the muffin is lopsided, then the heat is too high. If the top is weary, then the oven heat is too low. Remove muffins immediately from the pan and cool on wire racks. Muffins are never better than right out of the oven.

Muffins or their batter can be frozen, so make an extra batch. After cooling, wrap tightly in a plastic bag, squeeze out any air, and freeze. Defrost frozen batter and use as in the recipe. Frozen muffins can be defrosted, then wrapped in foil and warmed in a 450° oven for 5 minutes.

Excellent Corn Muffins

½ cup sugar
3 tablespoons canola oil
1 egg
1 egg white
1 cup skim milk
1½ cups all-purpose flour
½ cup yellow cornmeal
2 tablespoons baking powder
½ teaspoon salt

Serving: 1 Muffin
Protein: 4 gm
Carbs: 26 gm
Sodium: 231 mg

Calories: 155
Fat: 4 gm
Cholesterol: 18 mg
Calcium: 110 mg

MAKES 12 MUFFINS

Preheat oven to 400°. Spray a large muffin tin with nonstick oil.

In a bowl, cream sugar and oil. Beat in egg, egg white and milk.

In a large bowl, stir together flour, cornmeal, baking powder and salt. With a few quick strokes, combine dry and liquid ingredients. Fill muffin cups ¾ full. Bake 20 minutes, or until a toothpick inserted into the middle comes out clean and tops are golden.

Remove from tins and serve hot.

Apple Gems

3 cups peeled and finely
    diced apples
1 cup sugar
1 cup golden raisins
¼ cup chopped walnuts
1 egg
1 egg white
3 tablespoons canola oil
2 teaspoons vanilla extract
2 cups all-purpose flour
2 teaspoons baking soda
2 teaspoons cinnamon
pinch of salt

Serving: 1 Muffin   Calories: 171
Protein: 3 gm   Fat: 4 gm
Carbs: 33 gm   Cholesterol: 12 mg
Sodium: 155 mg   Calcium: 13 mg

MAKES 18 MUFFINS

Preheat oven to 350°. Spray a gem pan or large muffin tin with nonstick oil.

Mix apples, sugar, raisins and walnuts in a bowl. Let rest for 15 minutes.

In a separate bowl, beat egg, egg white, oil and vanilla until blended. In another bowl, stir flour, baking soda, cinnamon and salt together. Mix egg mixture into apples. Sprinkle flour mixture over apples and mix just until evenly distributed, although some lumps may remain. Fill muffin cups ¾ full. Bake 25 minutes or until a toothpick inserted into the center of muffins comes out clean. Cool for 5 minutes, serve warm.

Cranberry Nut Gems

2¼ cups all-purpose flour
½ cup packed brown sugar
1 tablespoon baking powder
½ teaspoon baking soda
1 teaspoon cinnamon
1 egg
1 egg white
4 tablespoons canola oil
1 cup nonfat buttermilk
2 cups chopped fresh or
    dried cranberries tossed in
    ¾ cup sugar
5 tablespoons chopped
    walnuts

Serving: 1 Muffin
Protein: 3 gm
Carbs: 28 gm
Sodium: 114 mg

Calories: 165
Fat: 4.5 gm
Cholesterol: 12 mg
Calcium: 43 mg

MAKES 18 MUFFINS

Preheat oven to 400°. Spray a gem pan or large muffin tin with nonstick oil.

In a large bowl, stir flour, brown sugar, baking powder, baking soda and cinnamon until well blended.

In a separate bowl, beat egg, egg white, oil and buttermilk. With a few quick strokes, blend liquid and dry mixtures. Gently fold in cranberries and walnuts. Fill muffin cups ¾ full. Bake for 25 minutes or until a toothpick inserted into the middle comes out clean. Cool for 5 minutes and serve warm.

Three-Berry Bread

2 cups all-purpose flour
¾ cup sugar
2 teaspoons baking powder
½ teaspoon baking soda
pinch of salt
1 egg
1 egg white
3 tablespoons canola oil
1 teaspoon vanilla extract
1 cup lowfat buttermilk
1 tablespoon finely grated
    lemon rind
1 cup fresh raspberries
½ cup diced strawberries
½ cup blueberries
2 tablespoons flour

MAKES ONE 12-SLICE LOAF

Preheat oven to 350°. Spray a 9" x 5" loaf pan with nonstick oil.

In a bowl, mix together flour, sugar, baking powder, baking soda and salt.

In a separate bowl, beat egg, egg white, oil, vanilla, buttermilk and lemon rind. Lightly stir flour mixture into liquid.

Combine berries in a bowl and sprinkle with 2 tablespoons flour. Gently fold berries into batter, pour into pan. Bake 45 minutes or until a toothpick inserted in bread comes out clean.

Cool on wire rack before cutting.

Serving: 1 Slice
Protein: 4 gm
Carbs: 33 gm
Sodium: 145 mg
Calories: 182
Fat: 4 gm
Cholesterol: 18 mg
Calcium: 43 mg

While fresh fruit is always best, individually quick-frozen whole berries taste great in the winter.

Chocoholic Bread

4 oz. semi-sweet Bakers
    chocolate
2 cups all-purpose flour
1 cup sugar
2 teaspoons baking powder
½ teaspoon baking soda
pinch of salt
1 egg
1 egg white
1½ tablespoons canola oil
¾ cup lowfat buttermilk
1 teaspoon vanilla
1 tablespoon Grand Marnier
    liqueur
¼ cup chocolate chip
    mini-morsels

Serving: 1 Slice   Calories: 224
Protein: 4 gm   Fat: 6 gm
Carbs: 41 gm   Cholesterol: 18 mg
Sodium: 82 mg   Calcium: 39 mg

MAKES ONE 12-SLICE LOAF

Preheat oven to 350°. Spray a 9" x 5"
loaf pan with nonstick oil.

Melt semi-sweet chocolate in saucepan
over low heat. When melted, set aside.

In a mixing bowl, combine flour, sugar,
baking powder, baking soda and salt until
well blended.

In a separate bowl, beat egg, egg white,
oil, buttermilk, vanilla, Grand Marnier
and melted chocolate until well blended.
Gently stir flour mixture into liquid.
Fold chocolate chip mini-morsels into
batter, and pour batter into pan. Bake
45 minutes or until a toothpick inserted
in center comes out clean. Cool on wire
rack before slicing.

Rose Garden Bread

2 cups all-purpose flour
2 teaspoons baking powder
pinch of salt
¾ cup sugar
3 tablespoons canola oil
1 egg
1 egg white
1 cup nonfat sour cream
1½ tablespoons finely grated
    orange rind
1 teaspoon rose water
½ cup minced red rose petals
    (with white part removed)
2 tablespoons powdered
    sugar

Serving: 1 Slice
Protein: 4 gm
Carbs: 34 gm
Sodium: 104 mg

Calories: 191
Fat: 4 gm
Cholesterol: 18 mg
Calcium: 61 mg

MAKES ONE 12-SLICE LOAF

Preheat oven to 350°. Spray a 9" x 5" loaf pan with nonstick oil.

In a bowl, mix flour, baking powder and salt until well blended.

In a separate bowl, cream sugar and oil with egg, egg white, sour cream, orange rind and rose water until well blended. Gently stir flour mixture into liquid. Fold rose petals into batter and pour batter into pan. Bake 45 minutes or until a toothpick inserted in center comes out clean. Turn out onto wire rack to cool. Dust Rose Garden Bread with powdered sugar before serving.

*Be sure to select edible
unsprayed rose petals.*

All About Tea Breads

Tea breads, or tea cakes, are quick breads and like all quick bread batters require very minimal mixing when combining the liquid and dry mixtures. Just mix until the flour stops streaking, too much stirring diminishes the texture. Lumps may remain and are fine.

Bake tea breads in the center of a preheated oven, leaving at least 6 inches between pans. Check the breads 5 minutes before they are supposed to be done. Insert a toothpick into the center of the bread and when it comes out clean, it is done. Properly baked tea breads will pull slightly away from the sides of the pan.

Tea breads are delicious served warm, but most need to be cooled before slicing or they will fall apart.

The flavor of tea breads improves if wrapped in aluminum foil and stored for 24 hours before slicing. Before wrapping, they must be cooled to room temperature. If storing for a longer period, wrap the whole loaf in foil, put it in a plastic bag and freeze. If the bread is sliced before freezing, then it is an easy matter to take a slice out of the freezer and pop it into the toaster. Whole loaves keep well for up to 1 month, sliced loaves for 2-3 weeks. To use, warm loaf to room temperature, wrap in foil and heat at 350° for 5 minutes.

Apricot Orange Tea Cake

1 cup fresh orange juice
1 cup dried diced apricots
2 cups all-purpose flour
½ cup sugar
2 teaspoons baking powder
½ teaspoon baking soda
1 egg
1 egg white
3 tablespoons canola oil
¼ cup skim milk
2 tablespoons finely grated
    orange rind
1 teaspoon almond extract
3 tablespoons almond halves

Serving: 1 Piece
Protein: 4 gm
Carbs: 36 gm
Sodium: 134 mg

Calories: 204
Fat: 5 gm
Cholesterol: 18 mg
Calcium: 54 mg

MAKES ONE 12-PIECE CAKE

Preheat oven to 350°. Spray a 9" round cake pan with nonstick oil.

In a saucepan, boil orange juice, remove from heat and add diced dried apricots. Let rest for 15 minutes.

In a mixing bowl, combine flour, sugar, baking powder and baking soda.

In a separate bowl, beat egg, egg white, oil, milk, orange rind and almond extract. Add juice-soaked apricots, then briefly stir in flour mixture. Pour batter into pan, decorate top with almond halves. Bake 45 minutes, or until a toothpick inserted in center comes out clean. Cool on rack.

Lemon Blueberry Bread

½ cup packed brown sugar
6 tablespoons flour
6 tablespoons lemon juice
1 teaspoon finely grated
   lemon rind
½ teaspoon cinnamon
¾ cup sugar
½ cup skim milk
3 tablespoons canola oil
1 egg
1 teaspoon vanilla
2 cups all-purpose flour
2 teaspoons baking powder
pinch of salt
2 cups blueberries tossed in
   2 tablespoons flour
1 tablespoon finely grated
   lemon rind

Serving: 1 Slice   Calories: 229
Protein: 4 gm   Fat: 4 gm
Carbs: 45 gm   Cholesterol: 18 mg
Sodium: 93 mg   Calcium: 58 mg

MAKES ONE 12-SLICE LOAF

Preheat oven to 350°. Spray a 9" x 5" loaf pan with nonstick oil.

In a bowl, prepare topping by mixing together brown sugar, 6 tablespoons flour, lemon juice, 1 teaspoon lemon rind and cinnamon.

In a separate bowl, beat ¾ cup sugar, milk, oil, egg and vanilla until smooth. In another bowl, mix flour, baking powder and salt. Gently stir flour mixture into liquid. Fold blueberries and lemon rind into batter, then pour batter into pan. Crumble topping evenly over top of batter. Bake 45 minutes or until top has formed a thick golden brown crust and a toothpick inserted into center comes out clean. Cool on wire rack before slicing.

Sun-dried Tomato and Garlic Bread

2 cloves minced garlic
1½ tablespoons olive oil
¾ cup diced sun-dried
  tomatoes
2 tablespoons finely diced
  black olives
2 cups all-purpose flour
1 tablespoon sugar
2 teaspoons baking powder
1 teaspoon baking soda
¼ teaspoon dried basil
pinch of salt
1 egg
1 egg white
2 tablespoons olive oil
1 cup skim milk
¼ cup crumbled feta cheese

Serving: 1 Slice
Protein: 5 gm
Carbs: 20 gm
Sodium: 281 mg

Calories: 146
Fat: 5 gm
Cholesterol: 23 mg
Calcium: 89 mg

MAKES ONE 12-SLICE LOAF

Preheat oven to 400°. Spray a 9" x 5" loaf pan with nonstick oil.

Sauté garlic in 1½ tablespoons olive oil for 1 minute. Remove from heat, add sun-dried tomatoes and olives.

In a mixing bowl, combine flour, sugar, baking powder, baking soda, basil and salt until well blended.

In a separate bowl, beat egg, egg white, 2 tablespoons olive oil and milk until blended. Gently stir the flour mixture into liquid. Fold tomatoes, olives and feta cheese into batter. Pour batter into pan. Bake 45 minutes or until a toothpick inserted in center comes out clean. Cool on wire rack before slicing.

Lemon Chive Pepper Bread

2 tablespoons butter,
softened
2 tablespoons canola oil
2 tablespoons sugar
1 egg
2 tablespoons finely grated
lemon rind
4 tablespoons fresh lemon
juice
3 cups all-purpose flour
2 teaspoons baking soda
1 tablespoon coarse-
ground black pepper
1 cup lowfat buttermilk
4 egg whites
¼ cup diced fresh chives

MAKES ONE 12-SLICE LOAF

Preheat oven to 350°. Spray a 9" x 5" loaf pan with nonstick oil.

Cream butter, oil and sugar in a bowl. Beat in egg, then lemon rind and juice.

In a separate bowl, combine flour, baking soda and pepper. Briefly stir ⅓ of the flour mixture into the liquid mixture, then half of the buttermilk. Repeat process with flour and buttermilk and remaining flour. Do not overmix batter.

In a separate bowl, whip egg whites until stiff. Fold egg whites and chives into batter, then pour into pan. Bake 35 minutes or until a toothpick inserted in center comes out clean.

Cool on wire rack before slicing.

Serving: 1 Slice	Calories: 180
Protein: 5 gm	Fat: 5 gm
Carbs: 28 gm	Cholesterol: 23 mg
Sodium: 260 mg	Calcium: 19 mg

Orange Yogurt Crumb Cake

2 egg whites
2 tablespoons canola oil
2 tablespoons honey
2 tablespoons finely grated
  orange rind
2 tablespoons orange juice
¾ cup sugar
1 teaspoon orange extract
1 cup nonfat orange yogurt
1½ cups all-purpose flour
1 teaspoon baking powder
½ teaspoon baking soda
pinch of salt
3 tablespoons flour
3 tablespoons sugar
2 tablespoons chopped
  walnuts
½ teaspoon cinnamon
¼ teaspoon nutmeg
½ tablespoon canola oil
1 tablespoon orange juice

SERVES 12

Preheat oven to 400°. Spray a 9" x 9" baking pan with nonstick oil.

In a bowl, beat egg whites, oil, honey, grated rind, orange juice, sugar, orange extract and yogurt until smooth. In a separate bowl, mix flour, baking powder, baking soda and salt. Gently stir dry ingredients into liquid ingredients. Pour batter into pan.

In another bowl, prepare topping by combining the 3 tablespoons of flour and sugar with walnuts, cinnamon, nutmeg, oil and orange juice. Blend with a fork. Crumble topping over cake batter. Bake for 25 minutes until toothpick inserted in center comes out clean. Cool for 5 minutes on wire rack. Cut into squares and serve warm.

Serving: 1 Piece
Protein: 3 gm
Carbs: 34 gm
Sodium: 117 mg

Calories: 181
Fat: 4 gm
Cholesterol: 1 mg
Calcium: 50 mg

Peach Melba Coffee Cake

SERVES 12

1 egg
1 cup nonfat buttermilk
2 tablespoons canola oil
1 teaspoon vanilla extract
2 cups all-purpose flour
¾ cup sugar
1 tablespoon baking powder
½ teaspoon baking soda
1 teaspoon cinnamon
pinch of salt
1 cup raspberries
4 tablespoons sugar
½ teaspoon cinnamon
2 tablespoons peach
  schnapps
2 peaches, peeled, pitted
  and finely chopped
½ cup Grape-Nuts^R cereal
2 tablespoons chopped
  pecans

Preheat oven to 400°. Spray a 9" springform pan with nonstick oil.

Beat egg, buttermilk, oil and vanilla in a bowl until well blended.

In a separate bowl, combine flour, sugar, baking powder, baking soda, cinnamon and salt. Briefly stir dry mixture into liquid. Pour into pan.

In a blender, whip raspberries, sugar, cinnamon and schnapps to sauce consistency. In a separate bowl, combine raspberry sauce with peaches, cereal and pecans to make topping. Sprinkle topping over cake and bake 45 minutes or until a toothpick inserted in center comes out clean of batter. Cool cake in pan on wire rack for 10 minutes before removing from pan.

Serving: 1 Piece
Protein: 4 gm
Carbs: 42 gm
Sodium: 203 mg
Calories: 218
Fat: 4 gm
Cholesterol: 18 mg
Calcium: 61 mg

Chocolate Swirl Coffee Cake

6 oz. semi-sweet chocolate
1 teaspoon butter
1½ cups all-purpose flour
1 cup sugar
2 teaspoons baking powder
¼ teaspoon salt
1 cup nonfat sour cream
1 egg
1 egg white
4 oz. nonfat cream cheese
1 tablespoon skim milk
1 tablespoon nonfat
  powdered milk
½ teaspoon vanilla extract
4 tablespoons powdered
  sugar

Serving: 1 Piece
Protein: 6 gm
Carbs: 45 gm
Sodium: 151 mg

Calories: 242
Fat: 5.5 gm
Cholesterol: 19 mg
Calcium: 82 mg

SERVES 12

Preheat oven to 350°. Spray 9" x 9" pan with nonstick oil.

In a small saucepan, melt 4 oz. chocolate with 1 teaspoon butter over low heat.

In a bowl, sift together flour, sugar, baking powder and salt. In a separate bowl, beat sour cream, egg and egg white until smooth. Beat flour mixture into sour cream mixture until barely smooth. Drizzle melted chocolate into batter and draw knife through batter several times to make swirls. Slowly pour batter into pan. Bake 20 minutes, then turn out and cool on a wire rack.

In a blender, whip cream cheese, milks, vanilla and powdered sugar until smooth. Spread over cooled coffee cake. Grate remaining 2 oz. chocolate and sprinkle on top.